New England's GHOSTLY HAUNTS

This book is dedicated to Larry Gallagher, owner of Dill's Restaurant in Marblehead, Massachusetts, who has hunted ghosts in New England and Nova Scotia, and proved to be an all 'round spooky fellow.

Ghost ship *AMAZON, later named MARY CELESTE, whose captain and crew from Massachusetts, mysteriously disappeared — story on Ghosts At Sea, Chapter VII - painting by B. Allen Niff.*

Cover Photos: ISBN 0-916787-01-X

The Tavern, now Kennebunk Inn, Maine, and owner Arthur LeBlanc — The Joshua Ward House, now Carlson Realtors, Salem, Mass. — Screeching Lady Beach, Marblehead, Mass. — The Old Burying Point, Salem — Harold Cudworth of Wareham and his haunted violin — The haunted house-barge and Mike Purcell, Miller's Wharf, Salem — Devil's Bridge off Martha's Vineyard and the wreck of the City of Columbus, plus Indian rescue crew at Gay Head — photo courtesy of Peabody Museum, Salem.

INTRODUCTION

This is the second book in the Chandler- Smith Publishing House Classic Series on New England Mysteries. It is the only one in the sixteen book series that provided me a chill or two in the writing.

I don't believe I am any more or less superstitious than the next fellow, but I have always been keenly interested in unusual occurrences, unexplained incidents, and unsolved mysteries, especially those that took place in my native New England. I was born and brought up in Salem, Massachusetts where, less than 300 years ago, falsely accused and self-proclaimed witches instilled fear and mass hysteria into my home town and neighboring villages. Today, Salem and her neighboring cities, Lynn and Boston, have attracted self-proclaimed witches into our society. On occasion they will be written up in the local newspapers and they are accepted for what they are, or profess to be, but for the most part they are ignored.

Fortune tellers, like witches, are a minority group here in New England, but they have also obtained equal rights through attrition, and they are no longer persecuted. Their lot in the days of yore, however, was less brutal than that of the witches. They were merely asked to leave town; whereas a witch was either hanged or, in the case of Giles Corey, crushed to death with stones.

Ghosts, sea monsters, and visitors from outer space have not yet made it in today's society. A few people may accept their existence, but most scoff at their mere mention. I am not a scoffer, for I have met a ghost, or I think I have, about which I will tell you shortly.

New England is also ripe with sealore, but I have omitted the legend and collected only unusual factual stories that are well documented. During my 25 years of research, I have made some startling discoveries, such as the macabre fate of all ships given the name ATLANTIC, and the strange coincidence of the number 33 surrounding all New England submarine disasters. I have also added a couple of stories about eccentric people whose obsessions, personalities, or experiences, conflicted with the norm. I do not try to fully explain their madness, nor the reasons for any odd occurences. Neither do I attempt to solve the many mysteries presented here — — I leave these puzzling incidents for you to wrestle with in your own mind. I have merely collected some stories about local places that I know and love in New England. Some of these stories are humorous, others are terrifying, and most boggle the mind. I shall tell you about my own nightmare first — — to set the mood.

I
THE SCREECHING LADY OF MARBLEHEAD

When I was 16 years old, I moved with my parents from Salem to a seaside cottage in neighboring Marblehead, Massachusetts. I was already familiar with the legend of the "Screeching Lady", and the terrible murder that prompted the tale of her ghost walking the beach. The incident occurred on a rocky beach not far from the cottage we moved into near Peach's Point. The exact details of the incident have been lost through the retelling of the story by Marblehead fishermen, and the name of the woman who suffered such a cruel death on the beach has been forgotten. She was an English woman who was captured by Spanish pirates in the late 17th century, so the story goes, and was robbed of the valuable jewelry she wore, except for an emerald ring which was stuck on her finger. With even the utmost effort, the pirates could not pry it loose. All who were seized with this beautiful young lady had been murdered, but she was held captive.

When the pirates tried to raid the Marblehead fishing village, the captive lady, being for the first time so close to shore, attempted escape. She was pursued by the pirates as she swam ashore and was recaptured on the beach. Angry at not finding the riches they expected to confiscate at Marblehead, they brutally beat the young lady and cut off her finger in order to obtain the emerald ring. The woman was screaming frantically. Her cries could be heard by the fishermen and their families, who were hiding in nearby woods. After 30 minutes or so, the screeching ceased — the pirates returned to their ship and sailed out of Marblehead Harbor, leaving the young lady dead on the beach. The fishermen found her and buried her, but insisted that, on the anniversary of her death each year, they could hear her screeching over the wind.

After experiencing my first storm living at the waters edge in Marblehead, I could understand why the fishermen imagined they heard the woman screeching. Everything shakes and rattles inside the house during a Nor'easter; breakers roar onto the beach and the wind howls about the house, sounding like the hideous shrill of some poor spirit suffering unbearable pain.

It was in the early summer of my 20th year that I was confronted by an unwelcome caller in that seaside cottage, and the thought of this encounter still chills me to the bone. I vividly recollect the details of that May evening, for I have never had such a frightful experience before or since.

My mother and father had gone to sleep in their separate rooms on the other side of the house, and I had stayed up late in my room to study for an upcoming college exam. The wind outside was rattling the windows, but no storm was brewing and the sea outside my window was relatively calm. I had no thoughts of ghosts or the "Screeching Lady" — only the exam was on my mind. I snapped off the light in my room at about 11:30 p.m. and immediately fell asleep.

The sound of sleigh bells ringing louder and louder woke me. In fact, I could see the bells in my dream. I opened my eyes, thinking possibly the telephone was ringing in the next room. Then I heard someone approaching and assumed it was my mother. The bedroom door was closed, but there, standing in the doorway at the head of my bed, was an old woman wearing a long, white gown. Her ghostly face was cracked and wrinkled, her yellow hair flowed over her shoulders, down to her waist. She did not look at me, but stared straight ahead as if in a trance. I was so frightened that I could not move; when I opened my mouth to yell, nothing came out.

She entered into my room walking straight ahead along the length of my bed. When she reached the foot of the bed, she turned and faced me, but still did not look down at me. Her face seemed troubled, as I recall the apparition, and, like myself, she seemed to want to speak — but she did not utter a sound. She stood by my bed — a transparent old woman with long, stringy hair — as I, in numbed silence, stared up in terror. Finally, my voice returned and I roared defiantly at my intruder. She appeared startled and quickly turned to leave my room. I laid in bed, motionless for a few seconds. I was convinced that I had seen a ghost — possibly the notorious "Screeching Lady". Since my eyes had been open all the time, I therefore concluded it had not been a nightmare. I got out of bed, grabbed one of the knives from a collection I kept displayed on a nearby bookcase, and gingerly opened my bedroom door. What a knife would do against a ghost, I have no idea, but this was my first reaction — I wanted a weapon in my hand. When I entered the living room I saw nothing unusual. I walked through the house, only to find the old lady was nowhere in sight. Looking outside, I noticed there was a full moon.

At this point, you might conclude that the apparition was probably caused by my own mind working overtime, fatigued at studying for the exam; however, the story does not end here.

While searching the house for my ghostly visitor, now more angry than fearful at her intrusion, I heard my mother calling my name from her bedroom. I opened the door and found her sound asleep. I shook her awake and asked her why she was calling for me. She answered that she was dreaming and did not know why she was calling me. I then sat on the edge of her bed and told her of my experience. "That is very strange," she said, "for it was nineteen years ago this very day that your grandmother died. I was pregnant with you at the time," said my mother, "and your father's mother was an old woman who knew she was soon going to die. Her last wish was that she would see you before she died, but you were born six months later."

Was this a visit from my paternal grandmother? Or was it the "Screeching Lady" of Marblehead, who had experienced a horrible death on a nearby beach some 300 years earlier? I don't know the answer, but whoever she was, she thoroughly frightened me — and apparently I frightened her too, for she has never returned.

Screeching Lady Beach, off Front Street, Marblehead, MA

II
AMERICA'S FIRST GHOST

There are literally hundreds of ghosts whooping it up in New England. In fact, New England could claim to be the "Spirit Capital of America," considering the number of sightings and encounters that have taken place here over the years. You, however, must decide if the ghosts to whom you are about to be introduced are: (a) real spirits from beyond, (b) no more than products of old legends, (c) were created for some devious or mischievous reason, or (d) as Scrooge said of Marley's ghost, "the result of some undigested piece of beef."

For the past century or so, there have been groups and societies formed for the purpose of hunting ghosts and for visiting notorious ghostly haunts. Their mission is to either rid a place of poltergeists, or attempt to communicate some purposeful message to these spirits.

One of the first ghost hunters, and the founder of the New England Spiritual Society, was Britisher Arthur Conan Doyle, creator of Sherlock Holmes. On one of his occasional visits to Boston, before he developed an interest in ghosts, he said: "If there is an afterlife, and I doubt it, I'll cross that bridge when I come to it." Actually Doyle "crossed the bridge" before his death, when visiting Boston again, soon after World War I. His son had been killed in the War, and Boston spiritualist Mrs. Saule, during a seance, brought the son back for Doyle to see. Doyle later commented, "Every spirit in the flesh passes over to the next world, with no change whatsoever." — Seeing a ghost, usually changes a skeptic into a firm believer.

The first recorded and documented sighting of a ghost in America was in the year 1799 at Machiasport, Maine. It was on August 9th of that year that Abner Blaisdel and his family began hearing strange knocking noises in their seaside house. On January 2nd of the following year, Abner and his daughter heard a woman's voice from the cellar say that she was Captain George Butler's deceased wife, and that her original name was Nelly Hooper. David Hooper, Nelly's father, lived only six miles from the Blaisdels, so Abner sent for him. Old David was as skeptical a Yankee as you'd find anywhere in New England, but he trudged the six miles through drifting snow to see what was going on. Abner explained to David Hooper that his daughter's ghost had been around the house for some five months, and that he had no idea why she had chosen his house to haunt, and not her husband's or her father's house. David and Abner went into the cellar and the voice was heard again. Old Mr. Hooper became an immediate believer. He asked the voice questions to which only he and his dead daughter knew the answers, and she replied to his satisfaction. "I believe it was her voice," David Hooper later wrote. "She gave such clear and irresistible tokens of her being the spirit of my own daughter as gave me no less satisfaction than admiration and delight."

The first to see Nelly Hooper Butler's ghost was Paul Blaisdel, Abner's son, as he walked across the fields behind the Blaisdel house, only a few days after David Hooper's visit. Paul was so terrified that he ran home and reported that the apparition "floated over the fields." The next night, the voice in the cellar was heard again. This time, the ghost of Nelly Butler was furious and she gave Paul Blaisdel a tongue-wagging for not speaking to her when he saw her in the fields the day before. By February, 1800 everyone in Machiasport and surrounding towns knew about Nelly Butler's ghost; many came to the Blaisdel home to see and hear her. Nelly apparently was a shy creature, for she disappeared for four months, avoiding the crowds.

She not only returned to say her piece in May, 1800, but appeared before some twenty people in Blaisdel's cellar. One of the witnesses described her as "a bright light," and another said, " she wore a shining white garment." "At first the apparition was a mere mass of light," reported one female observer, then it grew into a personal form, about as tall as myself . . . the glow of the apparition had a constant tremulous motion. At last, the personal form became shapeless, expanded every way and then vanished in a moment."

"Her voice was shrill, but mild and pleasant," reported another. Before the year was up, over 100 people had seen or heard Nelly Butler's ghost and gave sworn testimony to the local pastor, one Reverend Cummings. Cummings was becoming upset with his parishioners. He did not believe in ghosts and did not want them to. Reports were that Nelly always spoke on religious subjects, so Reverend Cummings had to be careful in condemning her. One statement made by Nelly, to which many testified, was: "Although my body is consumed and turned to dust, my soul is as much alive as before I left my body." When Nelly was asked by Abner why she appeared in the cellar and not in the upstairs living room where the audience could sit more comfortably, Nelly replied, "I do not want to frighten the children."

Reverend Cummings was losing control of the situation and he decided to confront Abner Blaisdel, who, he concluded, was the creator of this phony ghost. Walking through the fields to Abner's house, his temper boiling at every step, Reverend Cummings experienced a strange revelation which changed his attitude and his life. He saw a woman in the field, surrounded by a bright light. She was, at first, no bigger than a toad and then she grew to normal height before his eyes. "I was filled with genuine fear," the Reverend later reported, "but my fear was connected with ineffable pleasure." Nelly didn't say a word to Reverend Cummings — she didn't have to. He spent the rest of his life preaching around the countryside about the glories of life after death as experienced by Nelly Butler; and he wrote a book about her experiences and her words of wisdom, as testified to by over 100 people, including himself. After confronting Reverend Cummings, Nelly was never heard from or seen again — except for one little incident reported by Captain George Butler, Nelly's husband. She appeared to him one night and gave him a terrible tongue lashing for remarrying, especially since he had promised her, on her death bed, that he would never marry another.

Like Nelly, some Maine ghosts apparently have a difficult time with size perspective. The ghost of Margaret Hutton, who appeared in 1972 to Carol and Bob Shulter at Port Clyde, Maine, also first appeared as a little person, only a few inches high, and then grew immediately to what is considered by flesh-and-blood humans as normal ghost size. Only a few days after Carol and Bob had moved into their new old-colonial home, Bob complained that he heard noises and footsteps in the hallway outside his room. Then, something kept pressing down on the bedsheets creating indentations on the bed, as if someone had been sleeping beside him all night. At one point, something pulled his hair. One night, when Bob was away on business, Carol had her friend, Marilyn, stay with her in the house. It was early morning when Carol screamed and called for Marilyn to come into her room. Marilyn found Carol cowering under the bedsheets and, although Marilyn saw nothing unusual in the room, she did sense something strange. Carol had woken a few minutes earlier and sat up to turn on her light, when she saw a small bright figure of a woman at her window. The little glowing creature had her hands up to her mouth, and then she got larger and larger before Carol's eyes. "She wore a white nightgown but I could see through her," Carol later reported. "She got larger as she came towards me and she seemed to be giving hand signals," then she disappeared; that's when Carol hid under the sheets and called her friend Marilyn from the next room. When Bob Shulter returned home and heard his wife's terrifying story, he immediately called in professional ghost-exterminators from New York. Before confronting the ghost, the New York team researched the house to see if it had any prior unhappy or disturbed residents. They found that one of its first occupants was Margaret Hutton of England, whose husband skippered the schooner

CATHERINE that had disappeared off the coast of Maine in 1843. Could Margaret still be waiting for her husband to return, they wondered? One of the ghost exterminators approached the window where the little woman appeared, and in a kind, soothing voice, told Margaret to clear out, that her husband wasn't coming back and that if she looked around in the great beyond, she might find him there. The Shulters were never bothered by the ghost again.

There are many haunted houses in Maine, but one of the most popular is the Gideon Straw house in Newfield. This old delapitated dwelling, which, up to recent times, has been used as a hunting lodge, is supposedly haunted by Gideon Straw's daughter, Hannah. She, by all human and ghostly rights, should be, and probably is, disturbed by the goings-on in the house since her death in 1826. Hundreds of men have spilt beer and whiskey on her tombstone, and, if that were'nt enough, during the hunting season they ritually stand over her grave, swaying drunkenly to toast her spirit. They have also been known to make rude remarks and tell dirty jokes. This would be enough to stir any respectable ghost into a grumble — especially a 30 year old female. One can not blame Hannah for being buried in the kitchen of the old house. She may have requested it before her death, or maybe it was the desire of her mother, her husband, or father. Like it or not, for over 160 years, she has been lying under a corner of the kitchen floor, with a five foot metal tomb plate embedded over her, which reads: "SACRED to the memory of Mrs. Hannah, wife of Ira Chadbourne, who died March 2, 1826 — age 30. Blest are the dead, who die in Christ. Whose triumph is so great. Who calmly wait a nobler life. A nobler life shall meet."

Even before Darrell McLaughlin and his hunting crowd invaded the house in 1958, Hannah had made herself known to the Sweeneys, who had lived there before. Mrs. Martha Sweeney said that "terrible whining noises come through all the fireplaces." Darrell McLaughlin and some of his guests often saw Hannah at the window by the kitchen. "Hannah started coming into my bedroom and stroking my cheek," reported Darrell. This prompted him to sell the house to two schoolteachers, Bob Drafahl and Russ Fairbanks. The new occupants began hearing many noises for which they could not account. "At first I thought it was fun owning a haunted house," said Fairbanks, but after an incident last Spring, when the sounds of footsteps and slamming doors kept him awake all night with a gun in his hand, Russ put the Old Straw House back on the market. With the house vacated, Hannah may sleep in peace for a while.

III
MAINE'S HAUNTED INN

Four of us were on our way to Halifax, Nova Scotia, in April of 1981. We had driven up from Massachusetts in the afternoon to stay at the Kennebunk Inn, in downtown Kennebunk, Maine, to get a good night sleep and an early morning start on the Portland ferry to Yarmouth, Nova Scotia. Mike Chandler, Al Janard, and Larry Gallagher didn't know that the inn was haunted — I did.

Two old neighbors of mine from Salem, Massachusetts, Arthur and Angela LeBlanc, had sold their home in Salem and bought the decaying old inn two years before. With blood, sweat, tears, and the aide of family and friends, they revived the inn. As the recently published "Guide To The Country Inns Of New England," puts it: "It was on its way to becoming a memory when the LeBlancs rescued it." It was built as a home by Phineas Cole in 1791, after buying the land from the Storer family. In 1804, Cole sold it to Benjamin Smith; he, in turn, sold it to a Doctor Ross in 1895. Some 33 years later, a Mr. Baitler turned the home into an inn, which he called, "The Tavern." Walter Day expanded it in 1940 and made it the 16 room, family-style Kennebunk Inn. While restoring the inn and expanding it to 22 rooms in 1980, Arthur LeBlanc would periodically visit his old Salem home for rest and recuperation. It was during one of these visits that he mentioned to me that the old inn was haunted.

"Why do you think so?" I asked him, realizing that Arthur, a retired high-ranking Air Force officer, was not one to worry about ghosts. "At night I hear noises . . . grumblings from the cellar . . ." I laughed. "On occasion, a cold, chilling breath of air sweeps into the bar area . . ." I snickered. "In the morning I find bottles spilled, and bits of debris on the bar-room floor, after I've cleaned up the night before . . ." "One of your guests or employees is a lush, and sneaks down after you've gone to bed," I said.

"Well, it's more than that," Arthur hesitated, as if he didn't want to say more. "One of our waitresses was carrying a full tray of our crystal stemware from the diningroom the other day, and a glass from the middle of the tray popped up into mid air, hovered for a few seconds, then dropped to the floor. The waitress almost went into hysterics, and our luncheon guests, who saw it happen, were awe struck . . . Really, the glass just floated in mid air . . ." I looked at Arthur suspiciously, thinking he might be over-worked. "Really!" he shouted, "I'm not kidding you."

"Do you have any idea who the ghost might be?" I humored him. "Was there ever a murder or suicide in the old inn?" "Not that I know of," said Arthur. "We just kind of accept Cyrus as an unpaying guest."

"Cyrus?"

"Yes, Pattie Farnsworth, one of our waitresses, says she has a strange sensation every time she goes into the cellar food locker for supplies. She says that she thinks Cyrus lives in the cellar. She says that when she's down there, the name "Cyrus" keeps buzzing in her ear, so we call the ghost Cyrus. Only Angela, Pattie, and I dare to go into the cellar — The other waitresses won't go down there, because Pattie says Cyrus lives down there under an unfinished set of stairs that lead to nowhere . . . Apparently they were supposed to lead up to one of the rooms of the first floor, but the builder must have changed his mind, and the stairs just lead to the cellar ceiling . . . "Look," said Arthur, a bit perplexed, "I can tell that you don't believe me . . . Come up to the inn some day and see for yourself . . . I'm sure you and Cyrus will get along fine." Arthur said no more about his ghost that day, but a year later on that cool April afternoon, my three friends and I were in the lobby of the old Federal-Victorian inn, having arrived to spend the night.

Angela LeBlanc, Arthur's wife, greeted us, but she wasn't the warm, gregarious Angela that I had known back in Salem. "I'm devistated," she told us. "My chef, Jerry Goodwin, my pride, my joy, my friend, was buried yesterday. He was only 46 years old; had just gone in for a regular check-up, and dropped dead of cardiac arrest in the doctor's office."

She showed us to our first floor rooms, but her mind was on her dead friend. "He was more than an employee. He was part of the family," she told us. Gallagher got a single room next to the bar-lounge, Al Janard was in a room across the hall, and Mike Chandler and I had a double room beside Gallagher's. Angela, acting as hostess, was near tears and I felt we had come at a bad time, but "no," Angela assured us. It was good to have company in the creaky old inn, for it was early Spring and she had no other guests. She needed friendly conversation to get the death of Jerry Goodwin off her mind. Arthur, who had been dozing upstairs, also saddened by the news of his chef's untimely death, joined us later for drinks, in the tiny but quaint bar-lounge.

"Even if you've come just as a stop-off to catch the ferry to Nova Scotia, I'm glad you decided to stay here," Angela assured us.

"He didn't come for that," Arthur laughed. "He came to see Cyrus."

"Who's Cyrus?" came the simultanious response from Gallagher, Chandler and Janard.

"Cyrus is our ghost," Angela informed them, matter-of-factly.

Chandler and Janard's eyes widened, realizing that they had been duped by me to spend a night in a haunted inn. Gallagher could not have cared less. He didn't believe in ghosts, and wasn't about to believe now. Arthur, with a wry grin, relished informing me and the others on what Cyrus had been up to since I had last talked to him. Cyrus, according to Arthur, had been very active the previous year, playing little pranks on the employees. Angela informed us that he particularly didn't seem to like Dudley, the bartender. "See those four little hand-carved wooden mugs behind the bar?" she asked. We all nodded. "Made in Germany, very expensive," Arthur added. "One evening last August, one of those mugs picked itself up off the bar and gave Dudley one hell of a whack on the back of the head." Gallagher blushed, "Come on Arthur, you're putting us on?" "It's true," said Arthur, "the mug lifted up, as if raised by some invisible hands, then sailed across the bar to strike Dudley, and he had one hell of a lump on his head to prove it."

"There were customers in the room here, who saw it happen," Angela added. Chandler and Janard were convinced that Angela and Arthur were serious, but Gallagher remained the skeptic. Arthur took us on a tour of the cellar and showed us the unfinished stairway where Cyrus supposedly lived. Gallagher, a restaurant owner, was more impressed with the deepfreeze unit and the storage room than he was with Cyrus' hideaway. When we returned to the bar, another man — a stranger — was sitting on a barstool having a beer. Angela was talking to him. Arthur continued talking about Cyrus. "I just stopped by for a drink," said the elderly, well-dressed stranger. "I lived in this place for awhile, some 25 years ago . . . I heard you talking about Cyrus, he isn't still around here is he?"

"Cyrus is our ghost," Arthur explained, somewhat embarrassed.

"Cyrus was the night clerk when I lived here," said the stranger. Angela screamed. "You're kidding?" Arthur's face continued to flush, but now with a tinge of fear. "We just made up the name . . . I mean, we have no real reason to call our ghost Cyrus."

"Well," smiled the stranger, "Cyrus was here when the place opened, back in 1940, and he was getting along in years even then; used to have his desk in that room," the man pointed to behind the bar. Arthur was feeling chills now, for where the stranger was pointing, was directly above the unfinished stairway in the cellar. The stranger finished his beer and left. Arthur never even thought to ask him his name. Angela just kept repeating, "I can't believe it." Arthur sat silently, looking exhausted, with a sheepish grin on his face. Chandler, Janard and I were convinced, but Gallagher, who informed us that "Kennebunk got its name because it's full-of-bunk," still was not about to believe in ghosts. "It's just a coincidence," he said.

Al Janard didn't sleep well that evening. Once, when he got up to go to the bathroom, he felt such a chilling cold breeze about his ankles that he popped right back into the bed and threw the covers over his head, without fullfilling his mission. Mike Chandler got little sleep, for he heard a raspy voice moaning for help throughout the night. Yet, I slept in the same room and heard nothing unusual, except once when I woke, I heard Gallagher snoring in the next room. In the morning, Gallagher reported that he had slept well, without interruption from the ghost. This surprised us, for, without knowing it, Angela had given him the room behind the bar which once was the office of Cyrus the Night Clerk of the Kennebunk Inn, directly above the stairway that led to nowhere.

Arthur LeBlanc in the cellar of the Kennebunk Inn, at the stairway that leads to nowhere.

IV
NEW HAMPSHIRE'S GOOD GHOSTS

The most famous New England haunted house is the "Ocean-Born Mary House" in Henniker, New Hampshire. Actually there are two such houses — there is also the "Sea-Born Mary House" in Little Compton, Rhode Island. These two ghostly haunts with similar names have confused ghost hunters in the past, so let me clear up this mystery of the two houses by telling you the story from the beginning:

In the summer of 1720, the ship WOLF, packed with Irish and Scots immigrants, was sailing from Ireland to Portsmouth, New Hampshire. Approaching the New England coast, she was hailed down and boarded by a crew of pirates, the WOLF crew giving little resistance to the marauders. The leader of these Spanish pirates was a notorious cut-throat named Don Pedro. After robbing and harrassing all aboard the WOLF, Captain Don Pedro ordered his pirates to kill all the passengers and crew. As his orders were about to be carried out, the pirate captain heard the cries of a new born baby from below decks, so he countermanded his order. Although a murderer, Don Pedro had a superstitious bent, and he felt that Providence had interrupted his cruel deed through the child. The baby girl, born aboard the WOLF during the voyage, was brought on deck by her parents, James and Elizabeth Wilson for the captain to see. The parents were told by Don Pedro that, "if you will name the child Mary, after my loving mother, and if you will accept this roll of green silk to be made into a gown for the child's future wedding dress, I will spare the lives of all aboard." The Wilsons agreed — who wouldn't agree to those terms?

The WOLF and her passengers arrived safely in Portsmouth a few days later, and her immigrants became the first settlers of Londonderry, New Hampshire. It was here that their little savior, Mary Wilson, a freckle-faced redhead, grew up. At age 22, she married her childhood sweetheart, Tom Wallace, and her mother made a wedding gown from the green silk, which she wore that warm August day in 1742. The Wallaces had four sons. In 1760, Tom Wallace died, and Mary and her sons moved to Henniker, into what is known today as the "Ocean-Born Mary House." The house from which they moved in Londonderry, was later disassembled — board by board — and moved to Little Compton, Rhode Island, where it was reerected. Today it is known as the "Sea-Born Mary House."

Like the two houses, there are also two conflicting stories as to what prompted Mary to move to Henniker. Some historians believe that Don Pedro, who had retired from piracy, bought the Henniker house and persuaded Mary and her boys to come live with him. Others say that Mary's son Robert built the house in Henniker for his mother and younger brothers to live in. Whichever is true, there is little doubt that in 1781, an old Spanish gentleman, assumed to be Don Pedro, lived, for awhile, in the house with Mary. Also, many believe that the old pirate captain had buried his treasure in or near the house, where Mary could keep an eye on it for him. If so, Mary held up her end of the agreement for a long time, for she lived in the house to the ripe old age of 94. During her lifetime, Mary had many interesting guests at the house, besides Pirate Don Pedro. Daniel Webster visited her often, as did President of the United States Franklin Pierce, and, even General Lafayette stayed at the house and planted a tree in the front yard.

Since about 1830, owners of the house have dug up the yard and the cellar in search of Don Pedro's treasure. In fact, one owner ripped apart the kitchen in an unsuccessful attempt to find gold and silver. About 100 years later, the ghost of Mary Wilson Wallace started appearing around the house, so say previous owners. Mrs. Flora Roy, who lived in the house some 25 years ago, reported seeing Mary, with her long flowing hair, in the kitchen and continuously heard her footsteps on the stairway to the second floor. Flora Roy's son also reported seeing her, in spirit form, wandering through the house and rattling around in the spacious kitchen fireplace. Yet, Mrs. David Russell, who owned the house from 1960 to 1973, said she neither saw nor heard ghosts in the house for all that time. The present owners are a bit angry at Ocean-Born Mary, not because of her hauntings, but because neighbors looking up the dirt road to the weather-beaten house at the top of the hill, constantly see the ghost of Mary, or what they think is a ghost, plodding about the front yard. Some of the folks in Henniker believe Mary appears in a horse-drawn black coach every Halloween; some camp out on the doorstep of the house on October 31, waiting for her to arrive in her coach. All who live in the area will agree, the owners in particular, that flying objects bounce off the house on All Hallows Eve, usually as the evening progresses, but this is not Mary's doings. Those who come to see her begin to hoot and holler when she doesn't appear, and some of the disgruntled ghost-watchers have thrown rocks and other articles at the house, in their frustration at not being haunted. Mary doesn't deserve that kind of abuse, and neither do the present owners of the Ocean-Born Mary House. Mary was a beautiful person in life, and, if she does haunt the old house and its environs, there is no reason to assume that she isn't as warm and cordial in spirit form.

Another beautiful, friendly ghost of New Hampshire is Val Marston of Hampton. This wonderful little ghost came to my attention through Chandler Blackington, who, back in 1967, took my place as Director of Community Relations for the John Hancock Mutual Life Insurance Company, in Boston. "Blacky," like his father, is a marvelous story teller. His father, Alton Hall Blackington, produced a radio series, back in the 1940s entitled, "Yankee Yarns." It was through this radio program that the ghost of Val Marston came to light. During a broadcast on ghosts, Blackington was contacted by a Mr. John Robinson of Lynn, Massachusetts, who had recently been vacationing at Hampton Beach. He told Blackie that, "while out walking one morning with my wife and eight year old daughter, we encountered a ghost. We saw the figure of a little boy standing on the grass in front of an old white house. He seemed to be brighter than his surroundings," said Robinson, "In fact, he fairly glowed. My wife and daughter saw him too, and my daughter Edith cried, 'Daddy, daddy, that boy, I'm afraid'."

Mr. Robinson described the vision as a handsome smiling boy about twelve years old, with a dark brown curl falling across his forehead. He had bare feet, coveralls — with his hands stuffed in the pockets, a blue sailor's blouse and he wore a sailor's cap. He wasn't looking at the Robinsons, but seemed to be staring into space.

"Hello sonny, do you live here?" Robinson asked the ghost, and immediately he disappeared. "My solemn word, what I've told you is the gospel truth," Robinson said to Blackington. "My daughter was baffled and asked where the boy had disappeared to, and my wife was so upset at seeing the apparition that she couldn't say a word for quite some time."

"My Dad pursued the story," Blackie told me, "and he went snooping around Hampton to see if any town folks had seen the boy-ghost. Surprisingly, many had." A middle-aged couple named Sanborn owned the "old white house" where the Robinsons had seen the ghost on the front lawn. They admitted to Blackington that they had seen the little boy often, "with sunshine around him, like a halo." He had even come to the back door one day, with violets in his hand for Mrs. Sanborn, "but when my wife reached to take them," said Mr. Sanborn, "he and the flowers vanished . . . He's like one of our family."

Blackington went to Town Hall to trace previous owners and occupants of the house, to see if he could find clues as to who the little boy might be. There, he found the information he was looking for, and managed to piece the story together: The little boy was named Val

Marston, born Valentine's Day, 1879. He died October 12, 1890. He and his parents lived in the old white house near the Hampton railroad station. His father owned an old gun, which Val had gotten ahold of one day and started playing with, in the front yard.

The gun exploded in his hands, and, although the wound wasn't too serious, Val died of lead poisoning. Blackington also found out that Val had a brother who was still living in Hampton, and owned a barbershop near the beach. He went to visit Chester Marston. Chester said he had never seen the ghost of his brother, but knew of others who had. He showed Blackie a photo of Val when he was a baby, with the big brown curl falling over his forehead. Chester confirmed to Blackie that Val always wore a sailor's cap, because he wanted to go to sea when he grew up.

The old white house in which Val Marston lived was moved two blocks away in 1983, and I don't know why. Whether the ghost of Val Marston moved with the house, or remains at the empty lot, is not known either. However, recently a summer visitor to Hampton Beach, Marie Maguire of Lowell, Massachusetts, revealed-on the "That's Incredible" television program — that she had encountered a ghost while coming home from her nursing job at the local hospital one night. . . . "It was 11:15 and I heard a child crying; then, in the corner of the window, I saw a little boy in an old fashioned sailor suit, with curly hair . . . I was frightened and ran." Later, Marie's mother and younger sister revealed to her that they had seen the little boy ghost in the sailor suit many times before. Has Val Marston moved to Lowell? or does he remain in Hampton? Whichever, Val, like Ocean-Born Mary Wallace, isn't trying to frighten anyone. He has to be classified as a good, friendly ghost, who, like Nelly Butler of Maine, doesn't always wait until the Sun goes down to make an appearance.

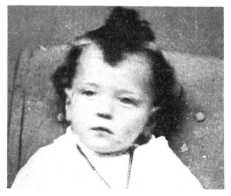

Val Marston

V
WHITMAN'S HAUNTED BED

David and Barbara English, with their year old son, moved to Whitman, Massachusetts from Delaware, in the Autumn of 1972. They moved into a quaint, 18th century Cape Cod cottage, on Temple Street, where they expected to live happily ever after. A few months after they had moved in, their good friends — a couple from Delaware — came to visit them. David and Barbara had little furniture and only one bed, but David remembered seeing an old bed folded into a corner crawl space in the attic of the old house. It was truly an antique with a carved headboard and intricately designed footboard. David pulled it out of the crawl space and set it up in a spare room. On the evening their guests arrived, the English's allowed them to use their room, and the hosts slept in the ancient bed in the guest room. David had a fitfull night and kept waking up with the feeling that someone was choking him. Barbara, on the other hand, slept soundly.

Next morning things began happening to Barbara. Her china teapot in the kitchen cabinet would not remain standing upright. As many times as she would stand it up in the cabinet, she would find it a moment later lying on its side. Then she stood there and watched after setting it on its base for the thirtieth time — she saw it rattle and tip over again. Also, all the coffee cups slid off their hooks in the cabinet. "I tried continuously slamming the doors of the cabinet for a long time one day," said Barbara, "just to see if the pot would fall over or the cups would fall off, but they didn't, because they couldn't." This convinced Barbara that there was either a ghost in the house, or some large truck kept traveling by the house and causing the pot and cups to tremble and fall.

David concluded, one evening, that Barbara's first guess was right; even though he didn't believe in ghosts. He found that the door to the attic crawl space, located near their bedroom, was always open — no matter how hard he tried to keep it closed. Barbara swore she hadn't been near the crawl space. Neither Barbara nor David could explain who or what could continuously pull back the latch and open the door to the crawl space; it certainly couldn't have opened by itself, and it was too high for their, now two year old, son to reach.

One evening, while Barbara was out bowling and David was puttering in the cellar, he heard footsteps upstairs. Thinking Barbara was home early, he went upstairs to greet her, but there was nobody there. This happened every Monday night in the English household, while

Barbara was out bowling — footsteps, but no one there when David investigated.

The incident that stimulated David into action, and thoroughly frightened him and Barbara, was when they invited a neighboring couple over one night to play cards. They played at the kitchen table, where David sat with his back to the upstairs stairway, while the other three could see it clearly. David's slippers were tucked between two posts of the stairway, where he could easily pick them up when he went to bed. Suddenly, the visiting couple and Barbara looked up in astonishment — the pair of slippers were floating in midair, and then they landed with a slap beside David's feet. One of their friends told them about a medium who lived in Brockton, who might help them rid the house of its ghost. David was somewhat embarrassed about asking a ghost chaser to come to their house, but when the Brockton spiritualist refused to come, David was angry.

His anger and fear increased a few days later, when he came home and found pieces of sandwich meat scattered over the kitchen floor. He shouted for Barbara, who was upstairs, and scolded her for messing up the kitchen. Barbara had left the slices of meat on the table only minutes before and it was too high for the baby to reach. David returned to Brockton and pleaded with the medium to come. The medium came, and, after sitting at the kitchen table for a few minutes, he asked Barbara and David to take him upstairs. He walked into the room where the old wooden bed which had been found in the attic stood, and he slapped the footboard with an open hand. Then he began mumbling. Soon, he was shouting, "You must go!" David then noted that the medium turned pale and looked as though he was going to faint. David and Barbara accompanied him back down to the kitchen where he told them what he heard and saw; although the Englishes had been standing beside him in the guest room they had neither seen nor heard anything unusual.

"The spirit is an old woman," said the medium, "who lived in this house over 100 years ago. She died in that old bed. Another old woman lived with her at the time," said the medium, "but did not aid your visitor while she was sick, and treated her quite brutally. She is very angry about this mistreatment, and, by the way," the medium added, "she does not like David."

The medium had insisted to the ghost that she leave the house and she, so he said, agreed. David and Barbara went to bed feeling a bit easier, but David did not sleep easy. Again, he felt that someone was choking him. Coughing and sweating profusely, he woke Barbara and they went downstairs. They sat at the kitchen table all night, and in the morning called the medium in Brockton. The medium was there at seven a.m., and, after going to the bedroom again, he told Barbara and David that the old woman's ghost had left, but returned during the night to choke David. The ghost intended to show David how she felt when she died in the bed by strangling on her own fluid, which filled her lungs. The medium suggested that the Englishs get rid of the bed, then the old woman was sure to leave.

That day, David sold the bed to a local antique shop, who, in turn, sold it to a ghost lover for over $100. David English, however, is happy to have the bed out of the house, and, although he now believes in ghosts, he sleeps soundly.

Harold Cudworth of Wareham, Mass. and his haunted violin.

VI

WAREHAM'S MUSICAL GHOST

Harold Gordon Cudworth repairs pianos and violins in Wareham, Massachusetts. He is also a talented violin player and owns a collection of 40 rare and valuable violins. The rarest and oldest in his collection is a Hornsteiner, made in Germany in 1769. One evening, back in 1945, Mr. Cudworth took down his Hornsteiner fiddle and bow and began playing Van Biene's "The Broken Melody." There came a tremendous rumbling from the kitchen, like the sound of a freight train; Cudworth stopped playing. He and his mother investigated and, concluding it was merely the gurgling of the kitchen sink, Harold continued playing the violin. The noise started up again, only louder this time; it wasn't the sink. It was a deafening roar coming out of nowhere, that would stop only when Harold Cudworth stopped playing his violin. When he tried playing a different tune there was no noise. Only when he played "The Broken Melody" did his kitchen rumble.

Cudworth is not a superstitious man, however, when, the following night, he again experimented by playing "The Broken Melody" on his Hornsteiner violin, articles such as coffee cups and sugar bowls started flying around the kitchen, and the weird, grumbling noise returned. Over the years, he has invited friends and relatives into his kitchen to witness this phenomenon; all are quite satisfied that the weird tune provokes strange happenings in the Cudworth kitchen.

A few weeks after the first incident, while playing "The Broken Melody" in his living room, similar loud noises came from upstairs in the house. When Cudworth went upstairs, the latch on the attic door jiggled four times. "Apparently my musical ghost just wanted to let me know he was there," Cudworth said later.

When Cudworth practiced in his upstairs room, his door latch wiggled when he played The Melody. In fact, one evening, he heard the bedroom door slam shut, but when he looked up, the door was open. These happenings were now beginning to wear on Cudworth's nerves. He was especially shaken another evening when, upon returning home from a meeting, he found his music cabinet open. He remembered closing it when he went out. Also, the music sheet sitting on top of the others inside the cabinet was "The Broken Melody."

It was a year later that Cudworth discovered that the musical ghost sometimes followed him. He was in New Bedford giving a young girl violin lessons, and, after the lesson, her father asked him to play "The

Broken Melody." Cudworth hesitated at first, but, since he was far from Wareham, he agreed and began playing the haunting tune. Immediately, the freight train sound that Cudworth had first heard in his kitchen was coming from the front hall of this New Bedford home. Then the front door began rattling until it sounded as though it was about to be shaken off its hinges. The man rushed downstairs to see who was trying to break down his front door, and Cudworth wisely decided to stop playing. In fact, he decided not to play "The Broken Melody" ever again.

In 1960, Cudworth was in Rochester tuning a piano and the little old lady for whom he was working knew he had his violin in the trunk of the car. She wanted him to play her a tune; she requested "The Broken Melody." Harold played, and found there were no noises this time, so he was satisfied that the ghost had either not followed him to Rochester, or had found some other musical instrument to haunt. When Harold completed the melody, the old lady said, "I've never had such a funny feeling in my life as when you were playing that tune. It was as if some spirit was standing beside me."

The townsfolk of Wareham had all heard of Cudworth's musical ghost. Every time he took his ancient violin from the case, he was prodded to play "The Broken Melody." In 1966, he was invited to play at a neighbor's house, whose living room was filled with nonbelievers. Harold began playing the ghost's song and, immediately, all the pictures and mirrors on the living room walls began swinging violently to and fro. The skeptical audience, now flooded with panic, begged him to stop playing, so he did — to the relief of everyone in the room.

Next day, the editor of the Wareham Courier got wind of the haunted violin and invited Harold Cudworth and his violin to the newspaper's editorial office. The editor and six typically skeptical reporters sat in the room and asked Harold to play "The Broken Melody." He obliged them; soon a stomping and grumbling sound came from the room directly above them. The editor assured all present that the room above was vacant, but the loud noises coming from it could not be ignored. Harold kept playing until, finally, the door upstairs slammed with such violence that the editorial room shuddered. Next, footsteps were heard coming down the stairs. One reporter grabbed a camera, swung open the door and flashed his camera. There was no one there: the photo once developed showed nothing unusual.

Harold Cudworth would like to know who his musical friend is; possibly the original owner of the Hornsteiner violin, or maybe Joseph

Hornsteiner himself — but Harold can't be sure. He's not even sure whether the spirit likes "The Broken Melody" or detests it, but whenever Harold wants a little excitement in life or desires to get a reaction from his friends and relatives, he merely breaks out his 18th century fiddle and plays that quaint old haunting tune.

The CITY OF COLUMBUS at her grave site, Devil's Bridge, Martha's Vineyard, January 17, 1884 - and below, the Indian rescue crew and their stove - in boat. Photo, courtesy Peabody Museum, Salem.

VII
WAREHAM'S GHOSTS AT SEA

Benjamin Briggs and Schuyler Wright were born and brought up together in the small village of Wareham, Massachusetts. Later, both became sea captains. Briggs was involved in what is believed to be the strangest sea mystery of all time, but there are many who believe Schuyler Wright suffered a more cruel fate.

The ship AMAZON, 282-ton and 100 feet long, was built in Nova Scotia in 1861. While on her maiden voyage, her skipper dropped dead at the helm. Six years later, the brig AMAZON was stranded on a reef at Cape Breton Island, Canada. She was salvaged and then sold to a New York shipping firm. On November 7, 1872, she cleared New York and headed for Genoa, Italy under her new name, MARY CELESTE. Her Captain was Benjamin Briggs of Wareham; and aboard was his wife, his two-year old daughter, and a crew of seven. The cargo in her hold was 1,700 barrels of alcohol.

Four days later, the ship DEI GRATIA, under command of David Morehouse, left New York for Europe. Off the coast of the Azores on December 4th, Captain Morehouse spotted the MARY CELESTE. She was under full sail, still heading for Italy, but she was cruising erratically. Morehouse sailed the DEI GRATIA alongside the CELESTE, and, seeing there was no one at the helm or on deck, he hailed Captain Briggs. He received no answer, so he and his crew boarded the MARY CELESTE.

There was not a person aboard, yet there was no sign of foul play. Everything was in order. Money, jewels, and other valuables aboard, most of which belonged to Mrs. Briggs, were in place. The CELESTE logbook was in good order, with the last entry on November 25th. The cargo was untouched and there were plenty of provisions and fresh water in the galley. Captain Morehouse and his crew did notice, however, that the ship's deck compass was broken and a lifeboat was missing from the rack. Otherwise, the CELESTE was "staunch and seaworthy." If Briggs, his family and crew, had voluntarily left the ship, Captain Morehouse could not understand why. He had sailed the same course as the MARY CELESTE and had not encountered any storms or heavy weather.

There have been many theories as to what happened to the ten people aboard the MARY CELESTE, but in retrospect, only one seems reasonably valid. The owner of the MARY CELESTE, James

Winchester, suggested that the alcohol cargo may have heated from the sun's rays and Captain Briggs, fearing an explosion, ordered everyone to abandon ship. The CELESTE then may have outsailed the lifeboat, which eventually capsized in heavy swells leaving all aboard to drown. The only question to this theory is: Why would the alcohol heat up? It was winter and the weather was cold.

The DEI GRATIA towed the MARY CELESTE to Genoa and the CELESTE was resold. An interesting sidelight to the mystery is that Captain Briggs' brother, Oliver Briggs, also from Wareham, Massachusetts, died on December 4, 1872 — the same day the CELESTE was found by Captain Morehouse. Oliver was captain of the brig JULIA HALLOCK that wrecked and sank off the coast of Africa.

The MARY CELESTE continued on as a jinxed ship for thirteen more years. Her new skipper was David Cartwright. While crossing the Atlantic from Europe to America, Cartwright came down with a fever and the CELESTE crew put him ashore at St. Helena Island, where he died seven days later. The next captain of the MARY CELESTE was Gilman Parker. He sailed her to Haiti with a cargo of furniture, but never made his port-of-call. The CELESTE hit Roshelle Reef in the Caribbean, and sank. Captain Parker and his first mate managed to escape and were picked up by a passing ship. Both men, however, were taken to court a few weeks later for allegedly sinking the CELESTE on purpose, to collect insurance money. No one ever determined whether Parker and his first mate were guilty, for both died mysteriously less than one month after the MARY CELESTE met her end.

Schuyler Wright, Bejamin Briggs' childhood friend from Wareham, became commander of the 2,000-ton, 270-foot long steamship CITY OF COLUMBUS. She steamed out of Boston on January 17, 1884, with 132 people aboard, heading for ports in Georgia and Florida. As the ship headed through Vineyard Sound off the Cape Cod coast, Captain Wright allowed his first mate to take the helm, while he went below for some needed sleep.

At that moment, many miles away at New Market, New Hampshire, Nathaniel Bunker woke up screaming from a nightmare. He dreamed that he was standing on a high cliff looking down on a large steamship as it hit a reef and began to sink. "I could see men, women, and children struggling in the water," he told two of his friends who came to visit him next morning. "Wreckage was everywhere, and I saw Lou

- 25 -

Chase trying to help my daughter into a lifeboat, but a big wave came and swept everything away."

Nat Bunker's two friends, who had found the old man sobbing in bed knew that Lou Chase had married Bunker's daughter only two days earlier, and that they were honeymooning aboard the CITY OF COLUMBUS. They, however, assured Bunker that his vision had only been a bad dream. "I know I'll never see my daughter again," cried the old man. Bunker's two friends could not understand how he could be so upset over a nightmare; but, that evening, they discovered that he was right — Bunker's daughter, Lou Chase, and 101 others aboard the CITY OF COLUMBUS were dead.

The steamship struck Devil's Bridge, an outcropping of rocks off Martha's Vineyard Island. Although the reef was properly marked with a buoy, the night watch aboard the COLUMBUS had not seen it in time. The startling crunch woke Captain Wright from a sound sleep. He rushed on deck and ordered the ship be backed off the reef, which put her in deep water with a large gash in her hull. Had Wright ordered the ship forward instead, she would have settled safely in shallow water no deeper than 12 feet.

"There was a grinding sound," reported one passenger, "and then I saw a woman with a baby in her arms. She cried 'save us,' but the sea embraced them and they were gone." More than 30 people sought shelter in the ship's rigging, but, a few hours later, they were found frozen solid to the shrouds and lines.

It was eight hours after the ship hit the reef that boats from Martha's Vineyard were able to make it through the heavy surf to the wreck site. Most of the boats were manned by Gay Head Indians, who heroically saved 29 people. Of the many women and children aboard the CITY OF COLUMBUS, only one 12 year old boy, George Farnsworth, was saved.

Schuyler Wright was accused of dereliction of duty and he lost his license as a ship master. He never returned to Wareham. Rather, he sadly spent the rest of his life as a laborer on the docks in Georgia. His restless spirit, however, say the Indians of Gay Head, Martha's Vineyard, now patrols the colorful high cliffs, directing ships around Devil's Bridge.

VIII
THE WILD GREEN MOUNTAIN BOYS

Almost every child has had an imaginary friend at one time or another during his or her growing years. I've often overheard every one of my four children talking in whispers in their bedrooms to someone who just wasn't there. I've occasionally interrupted them to ask who they were talking to, only to get the typical answer of "nobody," and I accepted that, as most parents do, considering it as part of child's play. In the hills of Vermont, however, there were two little boys, William and Horatio Eddy, who grew up with youthful spirits constantly about them that were anything but imaginary.

Neighbors often saw the Eddy boys playing in the fields beside their home in Chittendan, and there always seemed to be two other children playing with them, but when curious adults approached the boys, their playmates disappeared. At the Chittendan School, one teacher reported that, "loud penetrating noises followed them where ever they went, and in the classroom, items sailed across the room, thrown by unseen hands." The teacher, the school principal, and the other students, became so frightened by these mischievous unseen playmates, that the Eddy boys were expelled from school, never to return. Their father was furious that the state refused to educate his boys, and of course, the boys were elated, yet their mother seemed to take it all in stride, as if she fully comprehended the activities of her sons' poltergiest playmates.

Julie MacCoombs Eddy was said to possess supernatural powers, even before she gave birth to William, Horatio, and their two sisters in the mid 1800s. She was a remarkable fortune teller, the great-great granddaughter of Mary Bradbury, who was accused of being a witch during the Salem hysteria of 1692. She had been sentenced to hang at Gallow's Hill, but, with help of friends, managed to escape from Salem's Witch Dungeon. Julie married the evil-tempered Zephaniah Eddy in 1846, and moved into his rundown farm at Chittendan. As early as when the boys were infants in the cradle, friends and neighbors reported hearing whispers from unseen forces around them, yet the girls didn't seem to be endowed with this blessing or curse, or whatever it may have been.

As the boys grew older, although two years separated them in age, they looked like twins; chubby, black eyes, black hair, they were always solemn, unless frolicking with their unseen friends. Zeb Eddy loathed his sons and the unexplained occurrences that followed them where-ever they went. When the boys fell into deep trances, and strange utterances emitted from their lips, he would take them behind the barn and beat them unmercifully. Then, when the boys were about fourteen years old, Zeb hit on the idea that he could made a few extra dollars by exhibiting them and the strange spirits that surrounded them. He packed the family up and started traveling from town to town, first in Vermont, then Massachusetts, New York, and Pennsylvania. The boys would appear on stage, go into trances, and ghost of all kinds would be seen and heard dancing about them — Transparent children dressed as Indians, pirates, and soldiers, would whoop it up on stage as the Eddy boys stared into space. One little girl ghost was ever present during these exhibitions, constantly skipping rope around them. Zeb would allow skeptics to tie up his childrens' hands and feet, and even pour hot wax into their mouths, in an attempt to stop the ghosts and the grotesque loud noises that accompanied them. In some towns, such as Lynn and Salem, Massachusetts, the Eddy family was flogged by angry townsfolk and literally thrown out of town; in neighboring Danvers, young William Eddy was shot in the leg by a clergyman, who thought the boys were committing some sort of sacrilege.

When the Eddy boys reached adulthood, they refused to be exhibited in traveling shows, and because of their size, were no longer abused by their father. Yet, they were still tormented by the childish unseen spirits. Near the Chittendan farm, they often held seances at an eerie wooded section called Honto's Cave. They would summon up ghosts for anyone who was interested, including the ghost of Honto, the Indian for whom the cave was named. Some of these ghosts would sing or recite poetry, then they would disappear or melt away before everyone's eyes. Many psychic investigators, detectives, and probing skeptics came to Honto's Cave in an attempt to discover trickery or fraud; but, no one — to my knowledge — was successful in exposing them as imposters. Also it did not seem that the Eddy brothers had tried to make money from their hauntings.

Even the famous psychic Madame Blovatsky of Russia came to Vermont in 1873 to visit the Eddy brothers. Madame Blovatsky was a confidant of Rasputin, Russia's Mad Monk, who — more than Marx or Lenin — caused the Russian Revolution. She attributed her psychic powers to an explosion aboard the ship EUMONIA in 1870, while cruising from Greece to Italy. When the ship blew up and sank, with 400 passengers aboard, she was one of 17 who survived the calamity. From that day on she said she could see the future. Madame Blovatsky had made some marvelous predictions, including the two World Wars and the overthrow of the Czar, but the Eddy boys astonished even her. They had her dead soldier husband appear, for over a minute, before her at the entrance of Honto's Cave. Madame Blovatsky reported that, although the ghost of her husband didn't speak, "I have no doubts that it was indeed he in spirit form."

Were the Eddy brothers frauds, or did they really have the power to communicate beyond the grave? I have a tendency to believe the former, but the record of their unusual lives and achievements seems to indicate the latter. The farmers and other residents in and around Chittenden, Vermont, will give you a mixed reaction — Some believe, some don't, but many say that Honto's Cave is haunted. Probably the only way, today, to get to the heart of the controversy, is for you to spend a night at Honto's Cave. If you hear grotesque noises, or see mischievous ghosts dancing about the cave entrance, please let me know, because you won't see me there!

Portrait of Governor Thomas Dudley of the Massachusetts Bay Company in the 1630s. His harsh policies resulted in many hangings of innocent people, and possibly the curse of the Dudley family, the founders of Dudleytown, Connecticut.

IX
WHERE TO GO GHOST HUNTING

Probably the spookiest place in New England is Dudleytown, Connecticut, near Cornwall. While I was living in Connecticut in 1961, I visited the town, and from the moment I arrived I felt a strong urge to leave. I've never had such an eerie sensation, like someone or something was watching my every move from the nearby deep, dark forest. I wasn't alone of course, two friends, Mike Beltrami and Doug Campbell were with me. Although Doug kidded a lot about being in a ghost town, it was obvious to me that he was uneasy, and Mike was noticably unnerved — Mike hadn't really wanted to come in the first place. "I don't like it here," he kept saying, "it gives me the willies," but Doug wanted to poke around in some of the old cellar holes. It took us twenty minutes to find the town, walking down the old trail leading from Cornwall, but then we saw the partial remains of stone buildings nearly hidden by growth; the once active streets, now covered with bushes and shrubs; and then the many cellar holes. The foundations of many houses, a church, store, and a school, were found still standing, and Doug collected a few old bottles. Although the sun's rays were slicing through the branches overhead, the quivering dark shadows playing over the ruins had me constantly peeking over my shoulder, expecting, I don't know what. It was mid-afternoon in June, yet I was chilled. I, like Mike, didn't like Dudleytown, and suggested we leave. Doug reluctantly agreed, and we made our way back through the thicket to the car. By the time we reached the paved road, we were all sweating profusely. "Why was it so cold in Dudleytown?" Mike asked me. I didn't know. All I knew, at the time, was that it was once a thriving place with many prominent citizens. As we drove back to Hartford, I was determined to spend some time in the library to find out all I could about Dudleytown.

Abijah, Bavzillai, Abviel, and Gideon Dudley, four brothers, left England for the New World in the 1630s. Their great grandfather, Edmund Dudley, had been minister to King Henry VII, and President of the King's Council. He was caught stealing from the king's treasury, was convicted of treason, and had his head chopped off on August 18, 1510. Another of their relatives, Thomas Dudley, was elected Deputy Governor of the Massachusetts Bay Company, under Winthrop, and was four times Governor of the Colony, beginning in 1634. It was Thomas, a persistant Puritan heresy hunter, who instituted the harsh punishments of that religion, which directly resulted in the hanging of Quakers and accused witches in Boston and Salem. It is no wonder that the four Dudley brothers decided to settle deep in the Connecticut woods, and no wonder, too, that the Dudley curse pursued them into this remote settlement called Dudleytown. Other colonists followed the brothers into the woods, and Dudleytown began to prosper. In later years, each of the four Dudley brothers died a mysterious or tragic death (one being hacked to pieces by wild Indians), as, so it seems, was the fate of almost every citizen of Dudleytown.

One of the town's first prominent citizens was General Herman Swift. He was advisor to General George Washington, but went insane when news reached him that his wife had been killed by a bolt of lightening at Dudleytown. Dr. William Clark, who built a stately mansion in Dudleytown, was called away to New York one evening; upon his return home, a few days later, found that his wife had gone mad in his absence. Neighbors said that she had run hysterically from the house, screaming that ghosts and weird animal-like creatures were after her. When Dudleytowner Gersham Hollister was found brutally murdered in William Tanner's home on the outskirts of town, Tanner himself went insane, also mentioning demons and ghosts, saying that Hollister had been killed by some weird form of animal.

By the mid 1800s, the supposed sightings of ghosts and weird animals in the woods near the town, caused many Dudleytowners to pick up their belongings and leave for good. One who left was Mary Cheny, who married a man who ran for President of The United States against Ulyses Grant is 1872, but who was better known for making the statement, "Go West young man, go West." Mary married Horace Greeley, and wisely took her husband's advice, moving west of Dudleytown to New York.

Only one family, the Brophys, were living in Dudleytown by 1892, and John Brophy publicly stated that no ghosts or wild animals would cause him to move out. That year his wife died suddenly of unknown causes, and a few weeks later his two little children disappeared — never to be seen again. A week later his house burned to the ground, and John Brophy stumbled into Cornwall. He was raving like a maniac, shouting about weird green spirits and giant animals with cloven hooves that had tried to capture him.

Today, I know of no brave ghost hunter who would dare to spend the night among the ruins of Connecticut's notorious ghost town, and, as for me, I wouldn't visit Dudleytown again even in daylight hours.

Recently, a Connecticut newspaper headlined: "Ghosts Return to Phelps House." The article stated that the Federal-style mansion on

Elm Street in Stratford, now a home for the elderly, and the scene of numerous hauntings in 1850, was being haunted again by disruptive poltergeists. The old folks and the nurses on duty were complaining about strange noises, gurgling sounds, and unexplained knockings at night. Often, the emergency alarm would be sounded without reason, by unseen hands. The police, firefighters, and even psychic investigators, visited the Phelps House, but found no reason for the nightly disturbances. It was concluded that the occupants were just jittery about things that had gone on in the house, over 100 years ago.

Reverend Eliakim Phelps was returning to his home on Elm Street in Stratford after Sunday service, on March 14, 1850. With him were his wife, two sons, ages three and eleven, and two daughters, ages six and sixteen. When they entered the house, they found the interior in shambles. Furniture, food, and expensive china had been strewn around the downstairs rooms; the minister's first thought was that the house had been burglarized, until he entered the diningroom. He then concluded that demon spirits had entered his home. Displayed about the room were eleven life-sized dummies, carefully and cleverly woven from old cloth, and wearing Colonial clothes. Most of the dummies were posed in a kneeling position on the diningroom floor, as if praying to a hideous looking dummy dwarf that swung from the chandelier. The town selectmen and police were called in, but no one could explain the reason for such a macabre display.

From that night on, the minister, with the help of friends and neighbors, stood watch over the room. Inevitably, when they dozed off during their vigil, the dummy displays would change, sometimes with new figures being formed. Skeptical newspaper reporters were invited to spend the night in the Phelps House, where two witnessed candlesticks and fireplace utensils dancing about the diningroom. A New York Observer reporter wrote: "While I was there, objects lifted from the table and flew from one wall to another."

"In my very presence," wrote the reporter from the Bridgeport newspaper, "the elder Phelps boy was carried across the room by invisible hands and gently deposited on the floor. Also, a supper table was raised and tipped over when the room was empty of people . . ."

A month later, while the Phelps family sat for dinner at the diningroom table, they were pelted by fruit, vegetables, and kitchen utensils, until they were forced to leave the room. "When all the family was present in the room," said Reverend Phelps, "strange noises around us, like the rushing of wind, would force us to part company. These noises were especially strong when we were seated at the table."

From March through October, hundreds of dollars worth of furniture was smashed, including marble-topped tables, weighing hundreds of pounds, that were lifted from the floor, with not a person near them, then smashed into pieces as they were slammed back down. By October, 26 windows in the house were broken from objects thrown by invisible hands, and 34 cloth figures were found hiding about the house, most in praying or reading positions. Reverend Phelps said, "I have witnessed these manifestations hundreds of times within the walls of my home, and I know that in hundreds of instances they took place when there was no visible power by which these motions could have been produced."

After eight months of fear and agony, the Phelps family moved out of the house, never to return. Apparently the poltergeists did not follow them to their next home, but remained at the Phelps House, where the old folks who live there now hear things that go bump in the night or are rudely awakened by the blare of the emergency alarm, touched off by unseen hands.

Coincidentally, there is another haunted Phelps house in New England, the Porter-Phelps House of Hadley, Massachusetts, also called "Forty-Acres". Jim Huntington, who grew up in the 14 room Colonial house in the 1930s, reported that, "my brother and I often saw the ghostly figure of a woman wearing a frilly cap, usually standing at the living room window. I remember, as a child, becoming terribly frightened the first time I saw this woman come to my bedside and appear to be tucking me into bed. My brother also saw the ghost tucking in his sheets and blankets. . . " Upon mentioning the ghost to his mother, young Jim was surprised at her reaction. "Just ignore the ghost," she told him, "it's the same ghost who tucked me to sleep each night when I was a child."

The ghost of the Porter-Phelps House is supposedly that of Elizabeth Porter, who lived in the house in the mid 1700s. Her bed is still in one of the many bedrooms, and recent visitors to the house say that they saw the imprint of her body on the bed. Typical of haunted houses, door knockers rattle and bang without reason in the Porter-Phelps House, and the old hatch-type door to the attic is always found open, even after it has been bolted shut. The ghost of Elizabeth lingers in the house, say prominent ghost hunters, waiting for the return of her beloved father, Captain Moses Porter. He had left home, one day, to join in the French and Indian War and never returned. Another more fearsome ghost who has been seen prowling around the grounds outside the Porter-Phelps House, is a naked Indian called "Pontu". He was Captain Porter's faithful companion and guide, who had also left Hadley never to return during the war years.

Another wandering Indian ghost is "Mingo," seen frequently at Harland Road, Milton, Massachusetts, bordering the Blue Hill Reservation — He has also been spotted off the reservation at Barnstable, Cape Cod. Local residents living near the desolate Harland Road, complained of seeing ghostly apparitions and hearing strange noises emitting from the area late at night. They recently called in a team of psychic researchers, who spent an evening walking up and down the road in search of ghosts. Two members of the group, Elaine Favioli and Edward Ambermon reported seeing, "jelly-fish like blobs with discernible ears and mouths . . . One was a woman in a full length gown, we call Tori, and the other, a Unquity Indian, we gave the name, "Mingo," said Ambermon. Ironically, some seventy miles away, at the Barnstable House in Barnstable, Massachusetts, an Indian called Mingo and a young woman ghost in a gown, named Martha, have been reported periodically down through the last 200 plus years.

The Barnstable House, dating back to Colonial days, is an eatery and boarding establishment that has had many owners over the years. Less than three years ago, Rick Linstedt became its owner. "I'm not interested in ghost, and I didn't want to hear any of the stories concerning ghosts in this place," Rick told me one day in April of 1983, "but I did have a chilling experience soon after moving in here . . . I was sitting in my office on the second floor, writing some letters, with my golden retriever snuggled at my feet. The dog suddenly jumped up, arched its back and growled, staring at the door, then, the usually brave brute, ran to a corner of the office and cowered, whining like a frightened kitten and still staring at the door. This of course unnerved me, for the dog was there to protect me. When the dog, still cowering, made a beeline out the side door, I grabbed its tail and headed out with him. I didn't return to the office for hours after that . . . Also, Martha, in her flowing gown and high-buttoned collar has been seen around here from time to time since I arrived. One day a customer came running up to the front desk, obviously frightened. He asked me if I saw the woman in the next room. I told him that I didn't. 'She has no feet,' the man said. 'I saw her walk across the room, and then I noticed that she had no feet.' I, of course, went into the room to investigate, but saw no one. What bothers me though," concluded Rick," is, when we built a new floor in that room, we layed it a few inches higher than the old floor; it dawned on me that Martha, who's supposedly been around here a long time, would be walking on the old floor and not the new one, thus she would appear to have no feet."

At three A.M. on a cold December morning in 1975, The Barnstable Firehouse got a call that the Barnstable House was going up in flames. On the first firetruck that sped to the scene, were: Freeman Crosby, Bob Klun, and Charlie Matthews. Matthews said he saw a lot of smoke coming from the roof, but no flames. He and Klun got out a ladder and climbed to the roof of the house. The skylight, where smoke was pouring out, was open, which amazed the firefighters. There was no way the skylight could have been opened from inside the house, for the third floor door to the attic had been nailed shut, years before. They could find no fire, just smoke, so they allowed the smoke to clear out of the house and returned to the firetruck. A woman approached the firemen as they were about to leave. "Where's your dalmation?" she asked them, then she cheerfully asked them other questions which didn't seem to make much sense, and promptly disappeared. "She was about thirty years old, with shoulder-length brown hair," said Matthews, "and she wore a white wedding gown, with a high collar, a wedding train, but no headpiece." There were ten firefighters at the scene at the time, yet only four of them saw the woman in white. "Yet," says Matthews, "the others were so close to her that they could have spit and hit her." The Fire Chief, Bill Jones, told Kathryn Swegart, reporter for the Cape Cod Register, that, "all four men swore up and down that they definately saw something . . . This crew is very straight, and not in the habit of seeing ghosts." Rick Linstedt thinks it was Martha, looking for attention. Janet Johnson, who owned the house before Rick, does not believe in ghosts, but she too experienced unexplainable incidents — which has set her to wondering. One night, when a group of high school students were staying overnight in the Barnstable House, "and making a racket," says Janet, "I was awakened by a bright light in my bedroom — There was a great fire in my fireplace, burning wildly — It was impossible and illogical, yet it was there — It extinguished itself just as mysteriously, but only after the high school students sleeping upstairs settled down." On another evening, Janet walked into the dining room to see the old fashioned candle chandelier hanging from the ceiling, ablaze with light. "I snuffed the flames and left the room," she said, "but several minutes later I returned to find the flames flickering again — again I snuffed the flames — and four times that evening, when I returned to the room, the candles of the chandelier were lit." Was it merely spontaneous combustion, or was it Martha or Mingo trying to tell her something, or merely seeking attention. There are, supposedly, other ghosts at the Barnstable House: Captain Graves, who once lived there; Lucy Paine, who was drowned in the brook that runs under the house; and Edmund Howes, who hanged himself from a tree in the back yard, because he went bankrupt during the Revolutionary War. Guests and employees have spotted the shallow-eyed Graves in the cellar, Howes in the attic — that is probably why it was boarded up — and Lucy has been seen skipping around the dining room, in the early evening, just about dinner time. "There's a whole bunch of them around here," says Rick Linstedt, "and, as a woman who recently held a seance here told me, my guardian angel protects me from them, which is fine with me, for goodness knows, my dog is of no help."

In my hometown of Salem, Massachusetts, known the world over for its witch hysteria of 1692, there is a haunted house with ties to the witch horrors, and prankish ghosts that rival the activities of those who dwell in the Barnstable House. Indications that the house might be haunted came to light only two years ago, since, for many years prior to that time, the old house had been vacant. During Salem's on-going Urban Renewal Project of the downtown area, it was decided by the city fathers to rehabilitate and revitalize many of the city's old homes and buildings which, over the years, had fallen into disrepair. One handsome Colonial brick building which was restored to its original majestic grandeur, was the Joshua Ward House. It was built in 1784, five years before George Washington visited Salem and slept in the house. It was constructed on the foundation of a previous house, formerly owned by another George, George Corwin, the cruel High Sheriff of Essex County. Corwin was known for having tortured accused witches in the Witch Dungeon in 1692, arrested and imprisoned over 160 of his neighbors, and confiscated all worldly goods of those executed at Gallows Hill. He was not a well liked man, so, when he died in the early 1700s, his family buried him in the cellar of the old house. They feared, that if they buried him in a graveyard, the angry people of Salem would dig him up and tear his body apart. Many years later, his body was quietly dug up and moved to the Broad Street Cemetery. Joshua Ward, who built the house that stands on Washington Street and once overlooked the South River to Salem Harbor, was a successful maritime merchant and ship captain. The South River was filled in during the 1830s and the Joshua Ward House now overlooks a parking area called Riley Plaza. The house was bought by Richard Carlson, two years ago, to be used as an office building for his expanding realty business.

My sister-in-law, Barbara Cahill, visited Carlson Realtors in April of 1983, seeking their help in finding an apartment. She was seated in the front office of Sherry Kerr, when, while waiting for Sherry to get off the phone, she noticed a "strange looking woman" sitting in a large wing-backed chair in another front room office across the hall. Barbara had no idea that the Joshua Ward House was haunted, but she told me that, "the woman's skin did not look like flesh, but was almost transparent, like glass. — She looked like a mannequin, just staring into space, and, during the few minutes I was waiting for Sherry, she didn't move a muscle. Although other people were around, no one paid any attention to her. I got a very eerie feeling. She was weird, really weird, wearing a long grey coat with frizzled hair. . .but then Sherry was off the phone and I turned away, never looking back into that room. I thought about that woman for days afterward, still wondering if she was a real person or not."

Julie Tache, one of the realtors at Carlson, called me recently and asked me to come to the Joshua Ward House. "I'm afraid we have a ghost down here," she said. "Why call me?" I asked. "I don't like ghosts any more than you do," but my curiosity got the best of me and I went down to the Joshua Ward House, only a mile from my own home. Julie was upset, not frightened, but upset. "Every morning I come into my office, something has happened in here overnight," she told me. "Even though I lock my office door every night when I leave, either a lamp shade is turned upside down, or papers I leave on my desk are on the floor, just little things that unnerve me — until this morning, when I found the two brass candle holders on the fireplace mantle, turned upside down . . . and these two candles were on the harth." Julie handed me the candles. — one was in the shape of an S, and the other was bent back like a boomerang. "They certainly couldn't have melted into those positions . . . In fact, those candles have never even been lit. How could that have happened?" she asked me. I had no answer for her, unless the room became so hot overnight that the candles just wilted. "This room is always freezing," said Julie, "even in the summer, when others are dying from the heat, the corner of this room near my desk is abnormally cold." Then Julie told me that at night, "at least sixty times in the past two years, the fire alarm goes off and, of course, the fire department calls either Dick Carlson or me to come down here and shut it off. When I have to get up and rush down here, the alarm always goes off by itself as I round Riley Plaza; but every time Dick is called down here in the middle of the night, he has to come into the house to shut it off . . . What do you think of that?"

"I think the ghost likes Dick and doesn't like you," I laughed, but Julie agreed. That morning, she moved out of her second floor office and into another room, where she hoped she wouldn't be bothered by ghosts. I decided to contact Dick Carlson, whose office backs up to the room that George Washington slept in. There is a closet beside the fireplace, where Dick keeps his graphs, floor plans and zoning maps, rolled up and stuffed into cubby-holes. "One day recently," says Dick, "while one of my employees, Virginia Kohler, and I were discussing a house for sale, the phone rang and the gentleman on the other end of the line asked for a specific plan of property in Marblehead. I told him that I had the plan around here someplace, but it would take me time to find it. Before Virginia's and my eyes, a rolled up piece of paper came out of the closet and spread itself out on the floor before my desk . . . You might not believe this, but it was the plan the man on the phone wanted." I checked with Virginia. "The incident is still upsetting to me," she said. Dick Carlson also mentioned that one day, his mother, while working on the second floor, heard a tremendous thud overhead on the third floor and went upstairs to investigate. "There was no one on that floor at the time," said Dick, "but there was a chair in that room tipped upside down."

John Gagnon, the courier and clean-up man for Carlson Realty, was grabbed from behind on the stairway one autumn evening, while he was alone in the house. "I could feel the hand on my shoulder, weighing me down, but when I turned around, nobody was there," he said.

Another Carlson employee who told me of freezing cold breezes that pass through the rooms, melted candles, and fire alarms that go off when certain office doors are about to be closed, is Lorraine St. Pierre. During our conversation, she mentioned a photograph of one of the brokers, that was taken around Christmas time. "Dale Lewinski, using a Polaroid Camera, was taking head and shoulder shots of all the brokers to display on a Christmas wreath, as part of our decorations. Everything was fine, until she posed young Julie Tremblay, inside the front door, to take her picture. When the photo rolled out of the camera everyone gasped, and Julie commented, 'I know I take a bad picture, but what are you all so terrified about?' The photo was not of Julie at all, but of the ghost that haunts the house." Lorraine directed me to Julie Tremblay's first floor office, where she reluctantly handed me the photo and another photo of her that had been taken at the rear of the house, shortly thereafter, for the Christmas wreath decoration. There are plenty of good looking girls and women working in the Joshua Ward House, and Julie is one of the prettiest, but the first image that came out of that Polaroid camera certainly wasn't she. I left the house with both photos — which are reprinted on page 43 — and, also with no doubt in my mind that Dick Carlson and all his pretty employees have got themselves one ugly female ghost on their hands.

Salem, of course, because of its bizarre history is a splendid setting for ghosts and haunted houses. One such dwelling, open to visiting tourists, is the Ropes Mansion on Essex Street, two doors down from The Witch House where Witch Judge Jonathan Corwin, uncle of the cruel sheriff, lived in 1692. The stately 18th century white mansion, filled with rare furniture and antique china, was the home of Judge Nathaniel Ropes, who was a good friend of John Adams until the Revolutionary War broke out. At that time, the house was stoned by an angry mob, for Judge Ropes was a Tory, siding with the British. After breaking a few windows in the front of the mansion, the crowd dispersed when they heard that the judge was on his death bed, and in no way could he hinder America's call for independence. The judge died a few days later. Another member of the family, Abigail Ropes, burned to death in her second floor bedroom years later. A flame from the fireplace torched her petticoat, and, although she screamed for help, the servants said they didn't hear her. Some say that, passing the house late at night today, you can still hear her blood-curdling screams. Rick and Georgette Stafford, recent caretakers of the Ropes Mansion, who lived in the house, were only bothered periodically by ghosts. "The burglar or fire alarm would go off now and then," said Rick, "bringing the police or fire trucks, and occassionally a dish would be knocked over in the pantry late at night, but otherwise, the Judge and Abigail have been fairly quiet ... Of course, there is that photo of the ghost, sitting on the couch in the front hall ..." Rick gave me a copy of the photo, taken by a professional photographer who wishes to remain anonymous. He had been hired to take a photo of every room in the house, mainly for insurance purposes, and the ghost appeared when the photos were developed. The photographer says he didn't see the ghost when he was taking the photo. — The photo appears on page 47.

Diagonally across the street from the Ropes Mansion is the Salem Athaeneum Library. Salem's foremost story teller, Nathaniel Hawthorne, tells a haunting tale about the Athaeneum, not as fiction but as something he experienced. At noon, every week day, the young author spent an hour reading in the Athaeneum. Although the library was generally crowded, "the men abided by the rules and did not talk to each other, even in whispers," wrote Hawthorne. One regular, who Nat nodded to in greeting each day, was the eighty year old Reverend Harris. "He sat in the same chair by the fireplace, everyday, reading his paper." Hawthorne was saddened, one morning, to read that old Doctor Harris had died in his sleep the night before; but, when Nat entered the library that day, the old man was still sitting in his favorite chair by the fireplace. Instead of reading, he stared at Hawthorne, "and seemed about to speak." This apparition appeared to Hawthorne every day for five days, but on the following Monday, the chair was empty. Hawthorne was a shy person, and thought he would seem foolish asking others in the library if they too had seen the ghost of the old man. So, never having inquired, he never knew whether the others had seen him or if he alone had had the rare opportunity of viewing the ghost of the good doctor.

Nathaniel Hawthorne's most famous novel, "The House of Seven Gables," is a haunting tale that brings thousands of visitors to the old house on Turner Street, in Salem, every year. Local residents seldom visit the house. I'm ashamed to say that I haven't been inside the House of Seven Gables since I was ten years old, but I do spend a lot of time in and around the wharf area near the house. Directly across narrow Turner Street is Miller's Wharf. Last summer, a friend of mine, Mike Purcell, opened a fish food restaurant on the wharf. While visiting Mike, he told me he wanted to expand his little operation to an old house that stood next door at the head of the wharf. He had started to fix it up and asked if I would like to see it. I agreed to a cook's tour. The house, built as a summer cottage by sea captain Herbert Miller, in the last century, was truely rustic, with wide beams supporting the ceiling. I told Mike that I thought it would make a fine rustic extension to his wharf restaurant. Then, Mike took me up the rickety stairs to the second floor. It was void of furniture and looked like the inside of an old ship. "That's just what it is," said Mike, "an old ship . . . Miller salvaged a sea-going barge out in the harbor, brought it into the wharf, and then hoisted it up here to make a second story for his summer home." There was even a trap door in the floor, which had been the bilge of the old barge. "This will make a terrific restaurant," I told Mike, but someone from the wharf had called to him, and he didn't hear my comment. Then, from what was once the pilot-house of the old barge, a raspy, gurgling voice, sounding like a rusty door hinge, said to me, "get out of here." There was no one else in the room, and the voice had that eerie quality of coming from beyond the grave. I felt the heat of anxiety flood my face and body, but I didn't move. — Had I heard what I thought I heard, I wondered. I could see Mike on the stairway, and I knew it wasn't he that had spoken. Then, the voice came again, in a loud raspy whisper, "get out of here." I walked to the other end of the house, pushed Mike aside on the stairway, and walked out into the sun and salt air. "Well, what do you think?" asked Mike, close on my heels. "I think your place is haunted," I said. "Where did that old barge come from, and what was her name?" Mike didn't know. I called Helen Cooke, Herbert Miller's daughter, a few days later, and she didn't know either. Except for my experience in Marblehead of seeing a ghost, that was the first time I had ever heard one, and I hope it is the last. To put it more succinctly, to you believers and non-believers alike, I don't ever want to see or hear a ghost again.

Mike Purcell standing at the door of the old ocean-going barge, converted into the second floor of a dock-side house by Captain Herbert Miller, which is now, without doubt, haunted. Photo by Travis Smith.

The Joshua Ward House, front and back entrances, now Carlson Realtors, Washington Street, Salem, Massachusetts. The witch-hanging Sheriff George Corwin was buried in the cellar, and George Washington slept on the second floor. The Ghost that now haunts the house, seems to prefer the second floor room on the right in the lower, rear entrance photo.

Using a Polaroid Camera, Dale Lewinski, an employee of Carlson Realtors, took a photo of fellow employee Julie Tremblay, inside the Joshua Ward House — The above photo was the result. Dale had taken photos of all the other employees prior to taking this one of Julie. It was supposed to be a head-and-shoulders shot, like the one taken a few hours later of Julie, shown below. Did the female ghost that haunts the house decide that she wanted to have her picture taken too? Obviously, the photo above is not Julie Tremblay.

X
SALEM'S ONE-LEGGED GHOST

An old sea captain, so I'm told,
Lost his leg in the Spanish Wars.
His wife would often scoff and scold,
For they had no food or winter stores.
Each day he'd row to Baker's Hole,
To catch a fish off Salem's shores.
He used his leg as a rowing pole,
For the poor old skipper had no oars.
To feed his wife, his only goal.
To complain of him, her only chore.

Tied to his wooden leg so bold,
Were baited hooks and fishing lures.
When his boat began to rock and roll,
As a Nor'east blow from Baker's bore,
Down went the captain deep and cold,
His wife to never see no more.
The wife now had no food or coal,
And from her eyes the tears did pour.
All that was left to have and hold,
Was the wooden leg that washed ashore.

Before the midnight church bell's toll,
A vision appeared in the misty moor.
From quivering fog a form did mold,
In seaweed garb, and deathly gore.
She heard the haunting, mournful droll,
Then saw his ghost come through the door.
"I've come for me leg," she was told,
"I just want me leg, I want no more.
It's from me body this leg was stole.
I needs it, so I can walk like before."

"I'll put it to sea to calm your soul,
I promise I will, me darlin," she swore.
When she awoke, at rooster's troll,
A nightmare she thought, invaded her snore.
But when she picked up the leg, so old,
Salt water dripped to the cabin floor,
And seaweed enough to fill a bowl.
It gave her bones a chill to the core.

To the sea, she carried the peg and its mould,
To perform the deed, she greatly abhored.

Then, out of the hollow leg something rolled,
A Spanish dollar the captain had stored.
Then more coins dropped out, silver and gold.
"Hurrah!" cried the widow, "I'm no longer poor."
But too near the edge of the cliff she strolled,
And fell to the sea with the gold she adored.
Like a hand from the depths, a current took hold,
And carried her screaming off Salem's shores.
Then the captain pulled at her leg, I'm told,
Just like I'm pulling yours.

The Tavern, now Kennebunk Inn, Kennebunk, Maine, where the LeBlancs and their ghost Cyrus, will give you a night to remember.

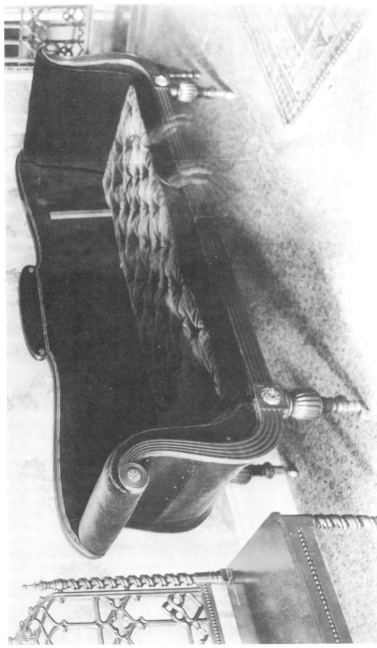

Photo taken inside Ropes Mansion, Salem, Massachusetts, where Judge Ropes haunts the rooms. Here the Judge sits for a spell on the front hall couch. After all, if you were wandering around this mansion for over 200 years, you'd want to sit for awhile, wouldn't you? The photographer says that no one was sitting on the couch when he took the photo.

- Blackington, Alton H., More Yankee Yarns, Dodd, Mead & Company, New York — 1956.
- Droney, James, Sale of Haunted Bed Ends Whitman Pair's Nightmare, Boston Herald American newspaper — July 23, 1973.
- Drake, Samuel Adams, A Book Of New England Legends and Folklore, Charles E. Tuttle Company, Rutland, Vermont — 1884.
- Cogswell, Leander W., History Of The Town Of Henniker, Republican Press Association, Merrimack, New Hampshire — 1880.
- Osgood, Charles S., And Batchelder, H.M., Sketch Of Salem, Essex Institute, Salem, Massachusetts — 1879.
- Robbins, Rossell Hope, The Encyclopedia Of Witchcraft And Demonology, Crown Publishers Inc., New York — 1959.
- Norris, Curtis B., Is Ghost Summoned A Critic?, The Boston Sunday Globe newpaper — August 28, 1966.
- Secretary, Commonwealth of Massachusetts, Pathways Of The Puritans, Plimpton Press, Norwood, Massachusetts — 1930.
- Smith, Frank, Ghosts And Poltergeists, The Danbury Press, Grolier Enterprises, Inc., Connecticut — 1975.
- Smith, Susy, Prominent American Ghost, The World Publishing Company, Cleveland and New York — 1967.
- Stevens, Austin N., Mysterious New England, Yankee Inc., Dublin N.H. — 1971.
- Swegart, Kathryn, Haunted Houses On Cape Cod, The Register Newspaper — August 27, 1981.
- Salem, Massachusetts Press, History Of The Town Of Hampton, New Hampshire — 1893.
- Yankee Magazine, House For Sale — "The Ocean-Born Mary House," Yankee Inc., Dublin, New Hampshire — July 1972.